America:
Stolen
Dreams

By M Baxter

For those who feel they have no voice, who died without ever having an opportunity, who lived with dreams stolen by the government they served and paid for.

"Our lives begin to end the day we become silent about things that matter."

--Martin Luther King

Table of Contents

The Dreams of All

The Color of Humanity

Where we are today

The Colonies

Reparations for Everyone, Except

Making the Case

Economics of Slavery

Freedmen's Bureau

Jim Crow Era

The Great Migration

Education and Homeownership

African-Americans and the New Deal

Where do we begin?

Conclusion

Our Options

The Proposal

References

The Dreams of All

> *"Prior to the institution of slavery, early African and non-white immigrants to the Colonies had been regarded with equal status, serving as sharecroppers alongside whites. After the institution of slavery the status of Africans was stigmatized, and this stigma was the basis for the more virulent anti-African racism that persisted until the present."*

> **Dinesh D'Souza, *The End of Racism***

No child is born with the stamp of failure in his/her future. They are all born, with the same opportunities and dreams. They are not born with prejudice in their hearts or with malice to man on their soul. They are not born with a name, physical beauty, a skin pigmentation, religious affiliation, sexual orientation or membership in any social-economic class. They are all born the same. Children are born a blank canvas for adults to write on, to guide, shape, nurture, name and to educate. It is the responsibility of the village to raise the child. We cannot and do not raise children in a bubble. They are influenced by many things in our society. Those influences can be the environment, economic conditions, siblings, parents, friends, classmates, teachers, religious figures, media and our government. It is the responsibility of all Americans to make sure every child has equal footing in acquiring the American Dream. It is our responsibility as adults to make sure all of the obstacles that we can control, economics, access to quality education and healthcare are available to all on a level playing field.

When a soldier goes into battle, the bullets don't determine who dies by race, gender, religion, socio-economic class or sexual orientation. The only time we seem to be equal is the day we are born and the day we die. The two things we don't seem to be able to control. We are all born from the womb and die with our last breath. In between this birth and death we treat each other as if we are different species of humans. Adults can't wait to add prejudice to the minds and souls of the young. It is an inherent character flaw that we as intelligent beings can't seem to overcome. We as adults refuse to sit down and think about the context of what we do and say to children, friends and strangers. It is as if we think we are born working towards whatever goal that is perceived as achievable in our own minds, without acknowledging that it takes everyone working together for this thing to work. Without consumers working, investing, buying, promoting, cheering, there would be no Oprah Winfrey, Bill Gates, Carly Fiorina, Warren Buffet, Lady Gaga, Leonardo DiCaprio, Denzel Washington, Tom Brady or Kobe Bryant. The people who toll every day that makes it possible for all of them to be successful are easily forgotten in our culture of hero worship. No great doctor or businessman can get to greatness without teachers and professors, sacrificing their dreams to ensure that they give students a quality education. You are not born with knowledge. You are not born a great entertainer or athlete in a particular sport. There are many people along the path of life who influence the direction of our lives. Some positive, some negative. What we do have as adults and members of this village called the United States of America is the ability to create an atmosphere of success. To tear down the barriers of prejudice which really have no bearing on our everyday life? As humans, if we can eat, get a drink of water and find adequate shelter that pretty much takes care of the basics of life. Everything else we do is an option that we can control with hard work and opportunities.

If we stop and think for a moment about the effect of our ancestor's actions. If we take a moment to look at policies that they have put into place in America, then we will see the barriers. It will help us understand that we must change the policies or like every great empire we will crumble. We cannot depend on the thoughts of men born in the 1700's to fix problems in 2016. The fore-fathers of the United States understood that people change, attitudes change, economics change and they wrote the Constitution as a living document that could grow with the country. They did not believe in co-mingling religion and politics, because they understood that human interpretation of religion is subjected to the opinions of men. The founding fathers knew that men could not be trusted with that responsibility and that a person's beliefs are an individual right reserved for each citizen. They did not want government coming into your home as it did in England and mandating your religious preferences. As most were Christians, they knew that slavery was wrong. They all had an opinion about it, but it did not stop them from the practice. Even from the writings of the first President, George Washington, he hoped at some point in the future of the new nation we would wipe out all remnants of the awful practice of selling and buying humans.

The Color of Humanity

With new data and science at our fingertips we are able to better understand our similarities as humans and our differences in skin pigmentation. There is a great youtube video, The Biology of Skin Color, by Penn State University anthropologist, Dr. Nina Jablonski, that gives a layman's example of the science of skin and the origins of man. Briefly for those who don't know, Humans originated in Africa. The African ancestors of all humans migrated north from Africa it is estimated over 100,000 years ago to the Middle East and the rest is history. The changing of the skin pigmentation is an adaption of a Humans location and environment and the need to survive based on both the effect of sun rays and available food sources. The skin pigmentation does not affect the biology of each individual Human as it pertains to knowledge. Every organ in the Human skeleton functions the same regardless of the skin pigmentation. The science of skin color confirms that we have a false sense of humanity towards each other. Based on tribal and racial segregation and it prevents us from moving on from this destructive legacy. When the laws of the United States of America are based on prejudicial policies based on skin color, it demeans the democratic process. It does not afford all of the citizens the equal rights that the constitution calls for and it inherently assumes that the laws being written based on that constitution are not to be taken seriously. Every word in the Declaration of Independence written after "all Men are created equal, that they are endowed by their Creator with certain unalienable Rights, that among these are Life, Liberty and the Pursuit of Happiness", is a lie. That all of the laws written based on this document are not to be respected or followed by those who are not representative of the government. President Abraham Lincoln stated that the "Government of the people, by the people, for the people", but that only seems to apply to a certain group of people.

The brown skin people who were brought here under the laws of slavery, then freed into the laws of Jim Crow that exist today, are not citizens of the United States of America. If they don't qualify for protection under all of the laws, then they are not citizens of any of the laws. As young brown men and women, descendants of the original humans die and suffer at the hands of a country that won't respect its own laws, how are we to expect their communities to ever flourish? What is the Color of Humanity?

"This declared indifference, but, as I must think, covert, real zeal, for the spread of slavery, I cannot but hate. I hate it because of the monstrous injustice of slavery itself. I hate it because it deprives our republican example of its just influence in the world, enables the enemies of free institutions with plausibility to taunt us as hypocrites, causes the real friends of freedom to doubt our sincerity, and especially because it forces so many good men among ourselves into an open war with the very fundamental principles of civil liberty, criticizing the Declaration of Independence, and insisting that there is no right principle of action but self-interest.

Peoria Speech, October 16, 1854, **ABRAHAM LINCOLN**

Where we are today

The purpose of this essay is to illustrate that the disparity in wealth between white Americans and people of African descent is no accident. It has been the purpose of the United States Government, since its acceptance of chattel (*noun*: a personal possession) slavery to exploit people of African descent, not just financially, but socially as well. We can trace the history of America and the United States Government and establish a pattern of laws put into place to maintain the African-American community in a second class status.

New York Times reporter Michael Powell wrote on May 17, 2010, "wealth begets wealth, and the lack of wealth perpetuates the same." Even if African-American families save at the same rate as white families they have less money to pay for college tuition, less money to invest in business and less money to tide them through rough times like the Great Recession of 2008. "The gap is opportunity denied and assures racial economic inequality for the next generation," Professor Thomas M. Shapiro writes from a study by the Institute on Assets and Social Policy printed in May of 2010. By extension I posit that this is nothing new. The economic gap between white Americans and African-Americans continues to widen even with the changes in the social status for African-Americans.

Let's take a look at history and some of the United States Governments actions to extend slavery and its effects beyond emancipation. A concentrated effort to deny economic, social and political equality to Africans-Americans and to stunt the growth of the African-American community through negative laws was in effect from the outset of slavery in 1619. The same forces to deny Africans full American citizenship that were imposed in 1619 are still in place in the United States of America in 2016. To see the pattern of discrimination a reasonable person needs only look at health care, criminal justice, sentencing laws, military draft during the Vietnam War, hangings and mass killings during the Jim Crow era and the lack of funds for the education of <u>freedmen</u> from the moment of emancipation.

The Colonies

In 1619 twenty Africans are brought by a Dutch ship to Jamestown Virginia for sale as indentured servants, marking the beginning of African slavery in Colonial America. During the Colonial era there were thousands of Africans and white Europeans serving European colonists for a term of indentured servitude. During this period of American history, indentured servants both white and African had opportunities to remove themselves from service. Sometimes if they just served a term of service, they would be granted freedom and a land grant. This illustrates a pattern put into place in the earliest days of settling America by wealthy landowners to find people to exploit for financial gain. This pattern of exploitation is still in place in 2016 America.

There were at least 40,000 free African-Americans in the Thirteen Colonies in 1770. They were either immigrants from the West Indies, descendants of early indentured servants or runaway slaves. They were faced with many challenges, stuck between being slaves and free white. They also had to navigate economic, social and legal restrictions, just as African-Americans do today. Before the American Revolution many African-Americans supported the country in fighting the British. Crispus Attucks, an African, is believed to be the first American killed at the Boston Massacre. Many Africans enlisted as Minutemen, both free and enslaved. Africans fought at Lexington, Concord and the Battle of Bunker Hill alongside white Patriots. Africans were lead to believe that if they joined the Patriots, they would either gain freedom or expand their civil rights in the formation of the new nation. During the Battle of Yorktown in 1781 it was estimated one quarter of the American Army was African.

The dream of freedom was not to be realized for the African-Americans during the Colonial era. The leaders of the Revolution were fearful that Africans serving in the military would stage an uprising. Slave-owners became concerned that military service would free their slaves, the economic backbone of their financial institution. The Continental Congress stopped the enlistment of slaves in 1775 and George Washington issued an order to recruiters, ordering them not to enroll "any deserter from the Ministerial army, nor any stroller, negro or vagabond".

The Patriots from Africa, who were loyal soldiers in the Continental Military, did not fare well after the Revolutionary War. The United States military did not honor the promise made to the African Patriots. In 1784 and 1785, Connecticut and Massachusetts banned all Africans, slave and free, from serving in the military. The United States Congress in 1792 formally banned African-Americans from military service only allowing "free able-bodied white male citizens" to serve. Many slaves who fought for the Patriots did receive their freedom, but most did not after their owners reneged on their promise to free them for service in the military.

According to historian Alfred Hunt in _Haiti's Influence on Antebellum America_, "President Washington issued $400,000 and 1,000 weapons to French colony Saint Domingue (Haiti) slave owners as emergency relief in order to put down the slave rebellion. The monetary relief and weapons counted as a repayment for loans granted by France to the Americans during the Revolutionary War." Sadly, part of the debt to France for helping win the Revolutionary war was paid for by helping to end a slave revolt in Haiti. This information confirms that the United States was formed with and by the sweat of Africans without compensation.

Reparations for Everyone, Except

rep•a•ra•tion   /ˌrɛpəˈreɪʃən/ Show Spelled [rep-uh-rey-shuhn]
Show IPA –noun

1. The making of amends for wrong or injury done: reparation
for an injustice.
2. Usually, reparations. Compensation in money, material, labor,
etc., payable by a defeated country to another country or to an
individual for loss suffered during or as a result of war.
3. Restoration to good condition.

        The Poverty & Race Research Action Council (PRRAC)
a civil rights policy organization convened by major civil rights,
civil liberties, and anti-poverty groups found that, "The
experience of American Indians in obtaining reparations from
the federal government should interest those who seek similar
actions with respect to Black Americans. American Indians have
received three types of reparations: (1) cash payments, through
the operation of the Indian Claims Commission and the U.S.
Court of Claims; (2) land, through an occasional action of
Congress to return control over land to particular tribes; and (3)
tribal recognition, by either Congress or the Bureau of Indian
Affairs. The first of these has been the least satisfactory,
measured by long-term impact on Indian communities. The
second was more satisfactory, but has been experienced by very
few tribes. The third, which is in process now, has had the best
results."

        They also established the Bureau of Indian Affairs under
the Department of Interior. The Bureau of Indian Affairs mission
is to: "… enhance the quality of life, to promote economic
opportunity, and to carry out the responsibility to protect and
improve the trust assets of American Indians, Indian tribes, and
Alaska Natives." With the creation of the Bureau of Indian
Affairs, the United States Government acknowledged that
policies instituted by the government had a negative effect on the
Indian community and it was the responsibility of the United
States government to reverse those negative trends.

An article published in <u>May 2011 in the Oxford Journal</u> states, "In 1952, West German Chancellor Konrad Adenauer met with world Jewish leaders and representatives of the State of Israel to formalize a program of restitution to be paid to Jewish victims of Nazism". German researchers have traced the origins of the reparations agreement to the intentions of German state legislators to introduce a law on the subject even during the period of military occupation, before 1949. Jewish researchers have credited the sustained efforts of various Jewish organizations with bringing about a restitution program. This paper argues that the United States played a significant role in helping realize a restitution program. The available sources on this aspect of US–German relations in that period reveal a determined course by the United States to push the emergent West German state toward a resolution of the Jewish restitution problem. Jewish organizations calculated that since absorption had cost $3,000 per person ($25,365 in today dollars); they were owed 1.5 billion dollars ($12,700,000,000 in today dollars) by Germany. An international commission under former US Secretary of State, Lawrence Eagleburger, has been trying to uncover the names of those who had been insured and died in the Holocaust. The World Jewish Restitution Organization was created to organize these efforts. On behalf of US citizens, the US Foreign Claims Settlement Commission reached agreements with the German government in 1998 and 1999 to compensate Holocaust victims who immigrated to the US after the war." Again the United States Government supported reparations for the injury caused to the Jewish community.

In 1942, in the wake of Imperial Japan's attack on Pearl Harbor, approximately 110,000 Japanese Americans and Japanese who lived along the Pacific coast of the United States were placed in camps called "<u>War Relocation Camps</u>". The internment of Japanese Americans was applied unequally throughout the United States. Japanese Americans who lived on the West Coast of the United States were all interned, while in Hawaii, where more than 150,000 Japanese Americans composed over one-third of the territory's population, 1,200 to 1,800 Japanese Americans were interned. Of those interned, 62% were American citizens. In 1988, Congress passed and President

Ronald Reagan signed legislation which apologized for the internment on behalf of the U.S. government. The legislation said that government actions were based on "race prejudice, war hysteria, and a failure of political leadership." The U.S. government eventually disbursed more than $1.6 billion in reparations to Japanese Americans who had been interned and their heirs.

Following President Ronald Reagan's example, it is time to offer reparations to African-Americans. The appalling actions of the American government towards Africans in America from its inception on the 4th of July 1776 and continuing today are based on "race prejudice, war hysteria, and a failure of political leadership." As stated by President Reagan. It is established that the United States government has supported polices to reimburse persons or people who suffered from the United States government injustices. The only difference between the people who have been reimbursed and Africans is the continuing bias against skin color and the United States governments stated policy by President Abraham Lincoln, that white Americans will never view Africans as equal American citizens.

"My first impulse would be to free all the slaves, and send them to Liberia, -- to their own native land. But a moment's reflection would convince me, that whatever of high hope, (as I think there is) there may be in this, in the long run, its sudden execution is impossible. If they were all landed there in a day, they would all perish in the next ten days; and there are not surplus shipping and surplus money enough in the world to carry them there in many times ten days. What then? Free them all, and keep them among us as underlings? Is it quite certain that this betters their condition? I think I would not hold one in slavery, at any rate; yet the point is not clear enough for me to denounce people upon. What next? Free them, and make them politically and socially, our equals? My own

feelings will not admit of this; and if mine would, we well know that those of the great mass of white people will not."

Speech at Peoria, Illinois October 16, 1854,
Abraham Lincoln

Making the Case

Let's talk about that last sentence in the <u>President Lincoln's speech</u>. It sums up the treatment of Africans from the end of slavery to the policies of the government of the United States of America in 2016. "Free them, and make them politically and socially equals?" Notice the question mark to end that sentence. Lincoln poses this question to America, then; he answers for himself and for the majority of Americans. Even those Americans after the Civil War who opposed slavery agreed with his assessment that it would not be possible for white America to accept the Africans as economic and political equals. "My own feelings will not admit this; and if mine would, we well know that those of the great mass of white people will not" said Lincoln. Even today the majority of "white people" do not believe that Americans of African descent should be equal politically, socially and economically.

To make the argument for reparations from the United States Government for the enslavement of humans based on the assumption that they were less than human and not deserving of protection under the American government, I think it must be established that the founding fathers who wrote the Constitution and the Declaration of Independence knew that the enslavement of humans from Africa was wrong and as such would deny a section of American society the benefits of the American dream. I want to state that African immigrants lived freely in North America before the implementation of the African slave trade and as such established that the founding fathers had knowledge of this and used the color of the Africans skin as a means to control their movements as slaves within the boundaries of the states. The founding fathers also conspired as would any criminal enterprise to achieve financial gain from the illegal transportation of Africans to the United States without due compensation.

"Slavery is such an atrocious debasement of human nature, that its very extirpation, if not

performed with solicitous care, may sometimes open a source of serious evils.

The unhappy man, who has long been treated as a brute animal, too frequently sinks beneath the common standard of the human species. The galling chains, that bind his body, do also fetter his intellectual faculties, and impair the social affections of his heart. Accustomed to move like a mere machine, by the will of a master, reflection is suspended; he has not the power of choice; and reason and conscience have but little influence over his conduct, because he is chiefly governed by the passion of fear. He is poor and friendless; perhaps worn out by extreme labor, age, and disease.

Under such circumstances, freedom may often prove a misfortune to himself, and prejudicial to society."

<u>*Signed by the order of Society*</u>*, **Benjamin Franklin, Philadelphia, 9th of November 1789***

Economics of Slavery

Jenny B. Wahl, Professor of Economics at Carleton College wrote in The Bondsman's Burden: An Economic Analysis of the Common Law of Southern Slavery, "Slavery is fundamentally an economic phenomenon. Throughout history, slavery has existed where it has been economically worthwhile to those in power. The principal example in modern times is the U.S. South. Nearly 4 million slaves with a market value of close to $4 billion lived in the U.S. just before the Civil War. Masters enjoyed rates of return on slaves comparable to those on other assets; cotton consumers, insurance companies, and industrial enterprises benefited from slavery as well. Such valuable property required rules to protect it, and the institutional practices surrounding slavery display a sophistication that rivals modern-day law and business." Professor Wahl's assessment that slavery had always existed to economically benefit those in power is just a confirmation that the ultimate goal for any country or society engaging in slavery, whether it was by color, ethnicity or social status was financial gain for those owning the slaves. The uniqueness of the American system of chattel slavery (slavery is a system of social stratification) is the fact that it was based solely on skin color and not whether Africans were deemed human. Americans and Europeans purchased African slaves from African slave traders or kidnapped African citizens on the continent of Africa. There is little history of Europeans or Americans venturing into the interior Africa to capture slaves. This confirms that Americans were well aware of the fact that African slaves purchased from the continent of Africa were humans of equal standing being purchased solely for the enrichment of the American economy without compensation to the individuals being enslaved.

In the South skin color dictated legal status. Humans who appeared of African descent were presumed to be slaves. In Virginia they passed a statute that actually classified people by race. Virginia was the only state to pass such laws in 1822 and essentially, it considered those with one quarter or more black ancestry as black. Some states in the 1800's used informal tests in addition to visual inspection: one-quarter, one-eighth, or one-sixteenth black ancestry might categorize a person as black. To bolster the case that Africans were disenfranchised because of skin color, free Africans enjoyed not much higher status than slaves except, to some extent, in Louisiana. In most states free Africans were not allowed to become Pastors, were prevented from selling certain goods, working as bartenders, had curfews, were not allowed to own dogs and many other laws to prevent them from achieving the American dream. In 1857 the Dred Scott case created the Federal law that prevented Africans from becoming citizens even though under the Constitution as humans and for some naturalized citizens, they should have been privy to those rights.

Professor Wahl writes further "Slaves faced the possibility of being hired out by their masters as well as being sold." Most of the slaves worked in manufacturing, construction, mining and as domestic servants. The slaves had the same legal responsibilities on the job, but none of the same protections as the white employees. If a white employee was injured on a job, they in general would receive some compensation for injuries, slaves could not. Most free workers had direct contact and arrangements with employers, unlike slaves. The slaves worked under arrangements between the slave-owner and the employer. A free worker could complain or walk off of a job because of conditions or issues with pay, a slave did not have this option. The law did offer substitute protections for the slaves. These protections were really for the slave-owners interest. The powerful interests of slave-owners showed they simply were more successful at shaping the employment law. Even in cases of harm caused to Africans and settlements in lawsuits for injuries, slave masters received compensation-not the slave.

Professor Wahl also bolsters the notion that it was the color of a human's skin that placed them at a financial disadvantage. She writes "Perhaps the most distinctive feature of Africans, however, was their skin color. Because they looked different from their masters, their movements were easy to monitor." With the ability to deny African slaves the rights of white Americans by simply using skin color to ascertain social status it was a cost effective way to distinguish between the classes of Americans. The ability to own property, acquire an education or the protection of rights through the court systems were just some of the rights denied the slaves. During the colonial period, slaves were able to acquire their freedom by converting to Christianity. It became difficult to decipher religious beliefs and far easier to establish skin color in relationship to class status. So the practice of freeing slaves based on religious conversion was ended. Some societies used long hair, markings or brands to denote slaves, yet skin pigmentation was less complicated and was a cheap way of keeping slaves separate from free Americans. As we now know skin color also served as an identifying mark for racists, even after the end slavery.

It is hard to pinpoint exactly how much America profited from the sale and use of Africans as slaves. In general, it has been determined that the rate of return was around 10 percent. It is also true that not only did slave-owners and traders profit from the trade and use of Africans, but the American consumer, and entrepreneurs reaped the benefits of the free labor. Consumers of products produced by slave labor enjoyed reduced prices for items and services. It also allowed American entrepreneurs to export items at a reduced cost, similar to our current trade imbalance with China and other cheap labor economies. Wall Street benefited by investing in plantations and free labor provided a wider profit margin.

> *"The true question is whether or not the Southern states shall be a part of this country. Is it wrong? Maybe. But, if the Northern states truly think about their interest, they will not oppose the increase of slaves because they will profit by selling the goods that the slaves produce."*
>
> *Founding Father - John Rutledge*
> *South Carolina*

Freedmen's Bureau

In the decade after the end of the Civil War, freed Africans were able to purchase land, participate in politics and acquire personal wealth. Most of this was accomplished under an unfunded program called the <u>Bureau of Refugees, Freedmen and Abandoned Lands</u>. After the Civil War, the American Freedman's Commission Inquiry stated,

> *"Offer the freedmen temporary aid and counsel until they become a little accustomed to their new sphere of life; secure to them, by law, their just rights of person and property; relieve them, by a fair and equal administration of justice, from the depressing influence of disgraceful prejudice; above all, guard them against the virtual restoration of slavery in any form, and let them take care of themselves. If we do this, the future of the African race in this country will be conducive to its prosperity and associated with its well-being. There will be nothing connected with it to excite regret to inspire apprehension."*

Now that sounds like a policy that would put Africans in a position to successfully integrate into free American Society. It shows that the politicians at that time understood that it would not be difficult to assimilate the Africans into free American Society if the country made an honest effort to be successful. We should read that statement again. It is powerful and if that policy had been implemented the history of America and African-Americans would be quite different. It was another promise to the African-American community left unfulfilled by the United States Government.

Congress got down to the business of writing a bill to aid the freedmen in the transition based on the recommendations of the American Freedman's Commission. The agency was to be named the Bureau of Emancipation. When the bill came up for a vote on March 1, 1864, Congress changed the name to the Bureau of Refugees, Freedmen, and Abandoned Lands. Because of objections from some in congress that the bill was exclusionary and aimed solely towards aid of Africans the name was changed to enlarge support for the bill. After a year of debating the bill, a compromise was agreed to and President Abraham Lincoln signed into effect the Bureau of Refugees, Freedmen and Abandoned lands on March 3, 1865. At the outset of the program, a key function was to provide rations to temporarily relieve the suffering of destitute freedmen and poor whites. A ration was considered enough flour, sugar and corn meal to feed a person for one week. The effects of the war, abandoned plantations, unemployment and poor crop yields made rations necessary for both freedmen and whites. Over 13 million rations in the first 15 months were issued. Over two thirds of the rations were issued to the freedmen. Such an enormous amount of aid being funneled to the freedmen and poor whites made the American population and the Freedmans Bureau uneasy and the program was ended in the fall of 1866. Even though the government knew that the aid was necessary, the government felt that the program would cause idleness. Opposition to government aid to African-Americans began here: At this time the idea of the lazy welfare bums became synonymous with the African-American community.

Even more daunting to the integration of Freedmen into the American society was a proclamation issued by President Andrew Johnson on May 29, 1965, that provided for reparations for Confederates. The proclamation conferred amnesty, pardon and the restoration of property rights for almost all of the confederate soldiers who would take an oath pledging loyalty to the Union. In order to continue the socio-economic disenfranchisement of the freedmen by the United States Government, Johnson supported the institution of Black Codes. These codes were instituted to bring Africans back to a position close to that of slavery; they also fought to have Confederate states accepted back into the Union without the condition of ratifying and adopting the 14th Amendment in their state constitutions. In essence, Africans were reduced to being slaves to not a single slave-master but to the state run system of exploitation. Despite the legal protection afforded by the 14th Amendment to the Constitution, these "Emancipated" slaves had no official recourse against discrimination.

The withdrawal of bureau officers was the beginning of the end of the Bureau of Freedmen. A Bill was signed into law on July 25, 1868 that required the withdrawal of officers of the Bureau and it stopped all functions related to claims and education. Barely 3 ½ years had passed between the ratification of the 13th Amendment on December 6, 1865 abolishing slavery to the law officially killing the Bureau of Freedmen. Africans who had lived under 200 years of slavery were now given minimal social and financial assistance in their new lives of freedom.

Even though the educational aspects of the Bureau were to continue for an indefinite period, Rev. Alvord, the General Superintendent of Education resigned his post on November 30, 1870. All activities of the Education Bureau ceased in March 1871. Some representatives in congress wanted to establish a permanent organization to assist the freedmen to help with relations between state and national governments. But the majority thought the idea too radical to override a veto by President Johnson, who was intent on maintaining second class citizenship for Africans. There was no enthusiasm to fund any government entity to allow for the equal integration of Africans into free American society. Just to be clear, this was a very important time of growth in the history of Africans in America and a continuation of their ability to assimilate. But of course those gains would not continue. Americans with the aid of Federal policy-makers thought that southern secessionists had suffered enough. At that point instead of funding programs for the freed slaves, the government put into place REPARATION POLICIES to reimburse white southern businesses, and farmers, men whose losses seemed far greater to the United States Congress than 200 years of enslavement.

After the closure of the Bureau of Refugees, Freedmen and Abandoned lands, African-American participation in politics was curtailed. The ability to acquire wealth and land diminished with the Black Codes. The PBS documentary, <u>Slavery by Another Name</u> explains Black Codes and Pig Laws,

"Immediately after the Civil War ended, Southern states enacted "black codes" that allowed African Americans certain rights, such as legalized marriage, ownership of property, and limited access to the courts, but denied them the rights to testify against whites, to serve on juries or in state militias, vote, or start a job without the approval of the previous employer. These codes were all repealed in 1866 when Reconstruction began. But after the failure of Reconstruction in 1877, and the removal of black men from political offices, Southern states again enacted a series of laws intended to circumscribe the lives of African Americans. Harsh contract laws penalized anyone attempting to leave a job before an advance had been worked off. "<u>Pig Laws</u>" unfairly penalized poor African Americans for crimes such as stealing a farm animal. And vagrancy statutes made it a crime to be unemployed. Many misdemeanors or trivial offenses were treated as felonies, with harsh sentences and fines. The Pig Laws stayed on the books for decades, and were expanded with even more discriminatory laws once the <u>Jim Crow</u> era began". Some examples of the continuation of the Pig Laws can be seen in the policing of Ferguson, Missouri, brought to light by the death of Michael Brown and highlighted by the Department of Justice investigation.

Jim Crow Era

Around the year 1830 a white minstrel performer Thomas Rice used blackface (charcoal paste) in performance of a song and dance called "Jump Jim Crow." Rice, known as "Daddy," used a young African-American boy or crippled elderly African-American man as inspiration for his character. Below are the lyrics from his song;

> "Weel about and turn about and do jis so,
> Eb'ry time I weel about I jump Jim Crow."

By the 1850's the "Jim Crow" character had become a part of most minstrel shows in America. The lyrics and dancing were used to depict African-Americans as inferior in popular culture. Jim Crow was synonymous with black, colored and Negro by white Americans.

With the Plessy v. Ferguson case the official beginning of the Jim Crow era was ushered in. This case reaffirms that the United States Government has participated in the disenfranchisement of African-Americans based on skin color and it has used laws and the courts to enforce it. On June 7, 1892, Homer Plessy boarded a car of the East Louisiana Railroad in New Orleans, Louisiana, bound for Covington, Louisiana, that was designated for use by white patrons only, as mandated by state law. Although Plessy was born a free person and was one-eighth black and seven-eighths white, under a Louisiana law enacted in 1890, he was classified as black, and thus required to sit in the "colored" car. When, in an act of planned disobedience, Plessy refused to leave the white car and move to the colored car, he was arrested and jailed.

At the end of the 19th century, acts of discrimination and segregation towards African-Americans were called Jim Crow laws and practices. In general, it is assumed the Jim Crow era started in the late 1890's. By 1910 every state of the former Confederacy had a system of legalized segregation and disenfranchisement. It was a continuation of white supremacy that predated the Civil War and was not exclusive to the Confederate South, but also practiced in the free North. The United States supported the Jim Crow laws with brutal acts and ritualized lynchings or mob violence against African-Americans. There were a reported 3,700 lynching of men and women from 1889 to 1930. The majority of the hanging riots were in support of white supremacy and in defense of segregation. In 1919 there were at least 25 of these race riots reported; in fact, 1919 was such a bloody year it is known as the Red Summer of 1919. Economic policies and conditions during this period were an attempt by America to ensure a separate but equal segregation between whites and Africans-Americans. It was to create a system that could exist within and outside of political and legal ramifications. The Jim Crow era encompassed written laws and unwritten laws, which continued even after the abolishment of Jim Crow policies.

That 1896 Supreme Court ruling (Plessy v. Ferguson) reaffirmed the United States government's continuation of African-Americans as second class citizens not privy to the full constitution. It reaffirmed a states right to enforce separate but not equal laws. It established that African-Americans by law are not allowed to their full earnings potential and are not allowed to petition the government or courts in cases of a grievance against American corporations and individuals based on the color of their skin. The Plessy v. Ferguson decision was not overturned until Brown v. Board of Education in 1954, a span of 58 years. That is approximately 182 years of sanctions imposed by a Constitutional United States Government on Africans in America. The official Jim Crow laws were not totally overturned until 1975. That is correct. A majority of African-Americans today were alive while Jim Crow era laws existed officially on the books. Even though we know that off the books laws are still enforce.

The impact of the Jim Crow era can be felt today in 2016 American society. Movies that glorify, African-Americans as victims waiting to be saved by white Americans or the United States Government are still in vogue and receive the most awards, The Color Purple, Precious, the Blind Side and in 2011

The Help. It is ironic that the first Oscar won by an African-American was for playing a maid in 1939 in Gone with the Wind. 72 years later, the movie with a large African-American cast, The Help, is receiving accolades for African-American women playing maids. It would be hard to find a movie portraying African-Americans as successful in American Society or even historical society that has received the same accolades. Halle Barry won an Oscar as a single mother waitress, saved by a white man and Denzel Washington won an Oscar for portraying a criminal police officer who is abusing a fellow white officer.

The case of the City of Baltimore against Wells Fargo in July 2011 is another example. Wells Fargo Bank is accused of using reverse redlining against African-American borrowers in majority African-American neighborhoods. Redlining is the practice of denying, or increasing the cost of services such as banking, insurance, access to jobs, access to health care, or even supermarkets to residents in certain, often racially determined areas. Redlining can be traced to the 1930's with the formation of the government sponsored Home Owner's Loan Corporation. The Redlining practices were soon adopted by private banks during the growth period of home ownership in America. The term "redlining" was coined in the 1960s by John McKnight, a Northwestern University sociologist. It describes the practice of marking a red line on a map to delineate the area where banks would not invest; later the term was applied to discrimination against a particular group of people (usually by race or sex) no matter the geography. During the heyday of redlining, the area's most frequently discriminated against were black inner city neighborhoods. For example, in Atlanta, through at least the 1980s, this practice meant that banks would often lend to lower-income whites but not to middle- or upper-income blacks. It is alleged that Wells Fargo knew that most of the families targeted in the Baltimore neighborhood would default on the bad loans. Wells Fargo was not concerned about the cost of the bad loans to the bank because most of the loans were sold to investors. Baltimore's city solicitor, George Nilson, stated,

"We're a majority African American community, and there are people in this city who take great offense when institutions take advantage of a community's historical lack of access to credit, and in some cases lack of sophistication, by putting them in loans they can't afford... It's offensive behavior and we shouldn't tolerate it."

Wells Fargo agreed to pay $85 million to settle the civil charges. The bank did not admit any wrongdoing. Associated Bank was required to pay out a $200 million settlement in 2015 by the U.S. Department of Housing and Urban Development for discriminatory lending practices to African-American and Hispanic clients.

The Great Migration

By the end of 1910 African-American progress was regressing. With the South suffering economically leading up to World War I, America began a shift in its economy to industrialization and the urbanization of southerners and African-Americans. With this transition came the Great Migration. Mass numbers of people moved from the farm economies in the South to the more industrialized urban areas in search of work. Of course Jim Crow Era laws followed African-Americans into the 20th Century during this migration from farm culture to industrialization.

With the rise of Northern labor unions to help more Americans move into the middle class during the 1910's and 1920's one might think that there would have been sympathy to the plight of African-Americans looking for work and opportunities. But again, another institution that was backed by federal law decided that African-Americans were not full citizens and as such not entitled to earn a living wage on par with white Americans or be entitled to the same protections from the federal government in the workplace. The relations between African-Americans and unions were antagonistic. Most of the unions in the North had explicit rules that barred African-Americans from membership. If an employer was faced with a union strike, they would hire non-union African-Americans, who were not likely to become members. There is evidence that African-American workers were used to break strikes in many labor disputes during this period.

During the 1930's African-Americans were entrenched in manufacturing and so were able to gain membership in the union movement. At the height of the Great Migration from 1916 to 1930, it is estimated over a million African-Americans migrated from the South to the North for better job opportunities. During this period African-Americans made substantial gains in employment in the manufacturing industries and as such gained power during the labor movement of that period. It is estimated the African-American presence in shipbuilding, meatpacking and the automobile industry between 1910 and 1920 increased from 500,000 to over 900,000 workers. It is important to note this period coincided with the United States' participation in World War I.

Education and Homeownership

During the early 1900's, the United States Government tried to implement policies to bring economic parity between the urbanized and industrialized South and the rest of the nation. These policies were instituted mainly to placate white southerners, but had no effect on the earning potential of African-Americans. Professor Thomas N. Maloney, Department of Economics at the University of Utah, writes in <u>Wage Compression and Wage Inequality between Black and White Males in the United States</u>, 1940-1960, "According to the Census, ninety percent of African-Americans still lived in the Southern US in 1900 -- roughly the same percentage as lived in the South in 1870. Three-quarters of black households were located in rural places. Only about one-fifth of African-American household heads owned their own homes (less than half the percentage among whites). About half of black men and about thirty-five percent of black women, who reported an occupation to the Census, said that they worked as a farmer or a farm laborer, as opposed to about one-third of white men and about eight percent of white women." It is clear that most African-Americans during the census of 1900 still lived in rural areas, were unskilled laborers, did not own a home and worked on farms as sharecroppers. Not much has changed in the way of homeownership for African-Americans in 100 plus years. In 2009 homeownership for African-Americans stood at 46%, compared to 75% for white America.

Is this yet another example of the written and unwritten policies and laws of the United States, having the effect to maintain the African-American community in a position of second class citizenship not privy to the rights and protections afforded by the constitution?

At this juncture in American history, the early 1900's, African-Americans were fighting to educate their children. The majority of African-American children during the 1900 census had never attended a formal school, even though it was 35 years after the Civil War. Jim Crow laws created a pattern within the education system to use tax dollars paid by African-Americans to help fund and promote the education gap between whites and African-Americans. The separate but equal laws that legalized segregated schools did not enforce the requirement of equality. Most of the resources or tax dollars during the Jim Crow era for education was funneled to white schools to increase the salaries for teachers, more funding for pupils and to reduce class size. Schools for African-Americans did not experience the same improvements. The end result was a sharp decline in the quality of education available to children in the African-American community. Ronald L. F. Davis, Ph. D writes in his essay, Surviving Jim Crow, "Many of the black colleges and normal schools serving African-Americans were hardly colleges at all. Because no public high schools for black children existed in most of the southern states, the typical black teacher's college included curricula at the secondary level." His point is that even with the opening of African-American colleges during the late 1800's and early 1900's, the level of education at most of the colleges was still only on par with the level of education at white high schools. If an African-American citizen received a high school education prior to 1910, it would have been from a church sponsored or private school which mostly existed in the North. Schools that did exist in the South were substandard, dilapidated shacks. African-American educators' salaries were well below the salaries of white educators. Most of the African-American educators did not have college training, especially in the South. Even today, Supreme Court Justice Antonin Scalia questions whether African-American high school students deserve to attend predominately white colleges and universities.

If schools were available in the South, most African-American families of poor sharecroppers had difficulty sending their children to school. Even in southern urban areas where at least 60 percent of African-American children attended school, the school year was shortened so that the children could work the cotton fields.

Dr. Davis also wrote,

"The Supreme Court's sanctioning of segregation (by upholding the "separate but equal" language in state laws regarding public schools) in the Plessy v. Ferguson case in 1896, and the federal government's failure to enact anti-lynching laws or to supervise voter election methods in the South, meant that southern blacks were left to their own devices for surviving Jim Crow. The lynchings, segregation, political disfranchisement, and economic impoverishment were compounded by the social humiliations of a rigidly imposed color line that dominated black-white relations. From 1876 to the 1960s, the story of that survival is one of great courage by African-Americans. It was a daily battle for one's life, self-respect, and basic civil rights. For most African-Americans, this struggle forged strength of character and an incredible sense of endurance that enabled them not only to survive individually but to prevail culturally as well. It is an epic tale of endurance and survival that ranks among the great, tragic feats of heroism in American and world history."

This is a very powerful statement and shows the courage and fortitude of African-Americans to continue to fight against a system that even today they do not understand. In 2010 the estimated poverty rate for African-American children was over 45%. For white children it was 14.5%. To make matters worse, we often hear the reframe that Minority students, especially African-American students receive scholarships over more deserving white students. That is an often repeated myth. White students on average receive over 72% of all scholarships. Minority students receive about 28% of available scholarship. So it seems we are still funding education for white children at the expense of minorities

African-Americans and the New Deal

During the Great Depression starting in 1929 many Americans were suffering. President Franklin Roosevelt tried to pass legislation to help Americans get back to work. Unemployment went from 4% to over 25 % in America and people were desperate for work. While most white Americans were suffering with job losses, African-Americans had to deal with discrimination, segregation, racism and job losses. Many leading New Dealers, Harold Ickes, Aubrey Williams, John Flores Sr. and Eleanor Roosevelt fought for African-Americans to receive some welfare assistance payments during this time. African-Americans were 20% of the poor in America, but they only comprised 10% of the population. The United States Government only allotted 10% of welfare assistance to the African-American community. White America received the other 90% of welfare payments during the Great Depression. Benefits allocated to the African-American community were small compared to the political and economic advantages of whites. African-Americans, even though they paid into the Social Security system, were denied benefits. The United States Federal Government did not enforce anti-discrimination laws in the South, since most African-Americans worked in agriculture and hospitality.

"The Social Security Act was also racially coded—in part because of the power of Southern Democrats in the New Deal coalition. Southern politicians, reported one architect of the new law, were determined to block any 'entering wedge' for federal interference with the handling of the Negro question. Southern employers worried that federal benefits would discourage black workers from taking low-paying jobs in their fields, factories, and kitchens. Thus neither agricultural laborers nor domestic servants—a pool of workers that included at least 60 percent of the nation's black population—were covered by old age insurance. *"*

Larry Witt
US Social Security Administration-2010

African-American troops who fought in World War II were not always able to take advantage of the G.I. Bill, specifically created to lift many Americans out of the Depression and to make housing and education more affordable. African-Americans soldiers were disproportionately discriminated in issuances of <u>Blue Discharges</u>. The blue discharge (also called a "blue ticket") was a form of administrative discharge created in 1916 to replace two previous discharge classifications. It was a very vague discharge and replaced the discharge without honor and the "unclassified" discharge. Of the 48,603 blue discharges issued by the Army between December 1, 1941 and June 30, 1945, 10,806 or 22.2% of them were given to African-American troops even though African Americans made up just 6.5% of the Army. Soldiers who received blue discharges faced problems getting jobs and were denied the benefits of the G.I. Bill for education and homeownership.

Even if African-Americans could purchase a home, the presence of African-Americans in a white neighborhood would reduce the property values as perceived by the United States Government. To combat this downgrading of white neighborhoods and to maintain economic superiority of white home values, The United States government created a policy to segregate the country. The policy involved making low-interest mortgages available to families through the FHA (Federal Housing Administration) and the VA (Veterans Administration). By law African-American families were entitled to receive loans from the FHA and the VA., but in most cases they were denied the loans because African-American neighborhoods were deemed in decline, even if the homes and neighborhoods were exactly the same as white neighborhoods. The rules for receiving the loans did not specify that black families could not get the loans, instead low interest loans would not be made to neighborhoods in decline. The exact wording in the policies did not appear to condone segregation, but it did have the intended effect of continuing the policies created with the implementation of Jim Crow laws. As proof that this policy denied homeownership to the African-American community and was officially sanctioned, the administration of the policies was under the New Deal. Most of the New Deal policies were put into place after World War II. The negative effects on the African-American community were that most white Americans after World War II were relocating to the suburbs and as such not affected by the rules against low-interest inner city loans. In addition, white families were encouraged to move to the suburbs by the offer of the FHA and VA loans.

Even state constitutions supported segregation. California had clauses on the books that gave local jurisdictions the right to determine where certain races of people could live. Even though the United States Supreme Court in the case of Buchanan v. Warley declared municipal resident segregation ordinances unconstitutional, white Americans formed Restrictive Covenant. A restrictive covenant was a formal deed restricting white property owners from selling properties in certain neighborhoods to African-Americans. To prove the connection between the United States Government and these policies, a white property owner who broke the agreement could be sued for damages by neighbors. It wasn't until 1948 in the case of Shelly v. Kraemer that the United States Supreme Court ruled that such covenants were unenforceable in court. Despite the ruling, a pattern of segregation was established in most American cities that exist to this day.

Where do we begin?

The information in this essay confirms the systematic exploitation of African-Americans before, during and after slavery by taking advantage of cheap labor and continuing their second class citizenship to keep them from realizing the American dream based on skin color. It is obvious that the United States Government and white America did not want African-Americans to achieve educational parity. If African-Americans were able to achieve an education, then the exploitation would be exposed. Many whites assumed that educated African-Americans would fight back against economic and social injustice. Some whites assumed that spending money to educate African-Americans was wasteful because the African-Americans were incapable of utilizing the education. A majority of whites also assumed that an educated African-American workforce would mean that they would lose jobs and opportunities, especially in skilled labor. Why do you think white Americans fight so hard against any policies that will lift the African-American community from its role of servitude? This is not a new policy, but a continuation of a policy put into place with the emancipation of Africans from American slavery. The ability of the United States Government to implement not only laws but policies to continue large scale abuse of the African-American community during the 20th Century would be considered brilliant if not for the fact that it was criminal, malicious and unethical under the Constitution signed into law by the founding fathers.

All the examples of our government's involvement in maintaining the second class citizenship of African-Americans are too numerous to include in this article. Michael Powell writes in Wealth, Race and the Great Recession, "The primal economic divide in America remains the chasm between the wealth of black and white families and it has widened steadily over the last generation." The data is irrefutable. A study by Professor Thomas Shapiro and his colleagues at the Institute on Assets and Social Policy at Brandeis University, involved data from studying 2000 African-American and white American families from 1983 to 2007. The data concluded that the racial wealth gap "has more than quadrupled over the course of a generation." The data points to a "stampede toward an escalating racial wealth gap." White American families saw "dramatic growth" in their financial assets. In 1983 the median value of assets for white American families was $22,000. In 2007 that ballooned to an average of $100,000. African-American families only experienced slight growth in wealth during this same period. Even at the higher income levels, middle-income white Americans accumulated $74,000 in assets by 2007. Higher-income African-American families during this same period only accumulated $18,000 in assets. Middle-income for both races was defined as $40,000 to $70,000 in 2007 dollars. At least 25 percent of African-American families in 2007 had no assets whatsoever to see themselves through the economic storm of the 2008 Great Recession. It is important to understand this data and it's long term effect on the African-American community. This is evident as Michael Powell wrote in his New York Times Article on May 17, 2010,

> *"In short, wealth begets wealth, and the lack of wealth perpetuates the same. Black families — who save at the same rate as white families — have less money to pay for college tuition, less money to invest in business and less money to tide them through rough times. This disparity in wealth denies African-Americans the opportunity for economic equality for future generations. The reasons for this gap are rooted deep in this nation's racial history. Government policy shut many blacks out of homeownership during the depths of the Depression. And during the post-World War II boom years, federal, state and city policies, and discriminatory bank lending and real estate practices steered even higher-income blacks to segregated neighborhoods and towns, where real estate appreciation lagged far behind that of predominantly white areas. Also, even high-*

income blacks most often hail from families of
humble economic origins. These families had
far fewer dollars to pass on to their children.
(As any young person who has cadged a down
payment from parents can attest,
intergenerational wealth transfers are a
particularly efficient way of gaining a foothold
in homeownership and so building wealth.)"

This statement affirms that the continued lack of opportunities for a majority of African-Americans to attain wealth, hold back the possibility of future generations to build wealth. African-Americans also suffer from the unbalanced Government tax policy. In the last three decades Congress cut inheritance and capital gains taxes, this policy keeps more money in the families who already have it, which is disproportionately upper-income white Americans.

Michael Powell also writes "There is finally the looming question of the toll taken by the recession. Certainly, many millions of white families have suffered grievously, losing houses and jobs. At the low point in 2009, white families had lost more than $1 trillion in wealth. But the recession fell even more heavily on blacks, as the average black family has far more of its wealth wrapped up in a home. (Whites, again for reasons of racial and economic history, tend to have diversified portfolios, with more stocks, pensions and the like.) 'Given differential employment rates, loss of wages, loss of health insurance, to the extent that all of these are worse for African-Americans, it has to make the wealth divide worse,' said William A. Darity, a professor of African-American studies and economics at the Sanford School of Public Policy at Duke University. All the arrows are pointing down. All of this data shows an urgent need of the American Government to alter its' policy in relation to the African-American community.

The next phase is to talk about the solution.

Conclusion

All of the laws, rules and disenfranchisement have created a group of people who cannot help the United States reach the next level in the global economy. We should be actively training citizens to fill highly skilled positions. Instead we look overseas for workers. What most Americans don't know about the United States Immigration policy is the use by American Corporations of the H-1B temporary visa. The visa is used to bring highly skilled foreign workers to the United States. Why? Because the United States of America refuses to nurture their citizens whose ancestors shed blood since the American Revolution to form the nation. The demand for H-1B workers by American Corporations still outstrips the current cap of 65,000 new H-1B visas that can be issued each year. In fact, from fiscal year 1997 to 2011, employers exhausted this quota before the fiscal year was over (except from 2001 to 2003, when the ceiling was temporarily increased). American Corporations are actively seeking to increase the number of H-1B visas. Can we afford to move more Americans onto the rolls of the unemployed while paying citizens of other countries to send American dollars back to their homelands?

Unless we change our policy towards African-Americans, try to right the wrongs of previous generations and put into place policies and procedures to allow them the American dream, this drag on the United States economy by the unemployed, underemployed and under-educated will continue. This shortage of educated citizens is taking us to a third world economy because we don't have enough people who can afford to purchase our goods and services. We are spending more funds on maintaining a privately financed system of slave welfare that does not put as much money into the economy as it takes out.

Our Options

Here are some options. As of June 2009, it is estimated that 905,800 African-American men and women were incarcerated in American prisons. That doesn't include all of the people on probation. The conservative cost to house a prisoner is $22,000 a year or $60 dollars a day. So a little math: 905,800 times $22,000 a year equals $19,927,600,000.00. That is one year only. To break that down by individual, it costs $132,000 per inmate for a six year stay at our fine institution of corrections (cost range from $13,000 upwards to $48,000 per year depending on the state).

Now let's look at the cost of education for that American, including 12 years of private school, 4 years of undergrad and a two year master's program. We will use a middle ground cost of $4000 a year for private schools grades 1 thru 12. That is a total of $48,000 to send that person to private school for twelve years. For four years of college with an average yearly cost of $9000 it is a four year cost of $36,000 total. For a typical Graduate school program we will use $26,000 a year for a two year cost of $52,000. The total cost is $136,000.

In terms of investments, if one spent $132,000 for six years of incarceration at an average of $22,000 a year, what is the return on that investment? To be generous an ex-convict will earn an average of $35,000.00 a year over a 10 year period. That equals $350,000. Not a bad sum of money. If the ex-convict is paying taxes into the system at a rate of 15% after deductions and exemptions, he/she would most likely pay about $45,000 in taxes over 10 years. Not much of a return on the initial 6 year investment of $132,000. At this rate it would take almost 30 years just to recoup the initial investment.

The second investment scenario to spend $136,000 over 16 years with an average of $7555 per year. The return on that investment? Taking a modest salary of a graduate with a master's degree and giving him/her an average salary of $70,000 a year over a 10 year period equals $700,000. Not a bad sum of money. If the graduate pays taxes into the system at a rate of

25% after deductions and exemptions, he/she would most likely pay about $150,000 in taxes over 10 years. A very nice return on the initial investment of $136,000.

What was not taken into account in this analysis is that it only cost $7555 a year to put the student through 18 years of school and college. Not only are the cost of the crimes reduced, but valuable members of society who actually put more into the system than they take out are produced. The cost of 12 years of public school for the ex-convict has not been included, a cost that we would never recover. The cost of public education over 12 years is almost $144,000.

If we take ideology out of governing, the numbers would start to make sense. We are past the point of punishing people for their skin color, place of birth, sexual preference, religion, socio-economic standing and prior prison sentence. We are all on the Titanic. Do we really want the ship to sink without a life vest for everyone? If we have the opportunity to load life vests on this boat for everyone shouldn't we? Or do we save some space in the hole so the wealthy can carry some toys on the journey, at the expense of the sinking ship and citizens without life vests? It isn't the fact that we don't have the money to save the ship and to purchase life vests for everyone. Can we afford not to invest in the future? If we continue on our present course, we will have more people being taken care of, than we have producing.

The Proposal

Here comes the difficult part: the investment.

There is no perfect formula, but there is a formula that we can use to determine who are considered descendants of slaves. If you can trace your descendants to the 1900 census, not born that year but an adult in that year, then you will qualify for the program to repay the African-American citizens for citizenship denial.

The first thing is debt. The African-American community is saddled with a debt by the United States Government that they cannot repay at this current rate. We have to fix 400 years of bad economic policy. We are also trying to help future generations acquire wealth, not debt. After saddling the community with hundreds of years of debt through taxes and overcharging for services and goods, now is the time to make it right. Making it right so that it benefits everyone is the most important thing. Let's put the buying power of the African-American community back to work helping America achieve economic success.

Incarcerated young men and women would not have to list a prior conviction on applications for employment unless a sexual offense. Americans would not be subject to credit checks when applying for job opportunities. If there are layoffs at a company, the last ones hired and the first ones fired policy has to be changed.

It would be to our great advantage as a nation if public schools could be trusted to educate African-American children but as we know that system has failed the community since its inception and cannot be trusted to ensure a quality education. We need immediate reform to ensure that the children are being educated. Modeling all school systems after systems that work is a no-brainer solution. Reforms in spending and awarding all education projects are important. It isn't the need for more money, but how the money is spent that seems to be the problem. Some may think it is impossible for African-American parents to participate in the education of their children. It is a myth. If the African-American community can see value in education they will find a way to participate. For some reason the African-American community is not given credit for fighting for educational equality for their children for the last 400 years against a system that continually tries to tell them it's impossible.

We cannot save everyone on the boat. Some Americans whose ancestors came to the shores after the 20th century have issues with whatever government that abused them before they landed here. Let's be clear, no other group of people in the United States of America has suffered the same injustice as the African-American community. But as with any other advances in Civil Rights for African-Americans, they too will benefit from the uplifting of the African-American community. By singling out Native Americans, Jewish Americans and Japanese Americans to give reparations for past wrongs, there was no consideration for any other groups wronged by our government. Why must African-Americans, who helped build this nation without compensation, be deprived of the opportunity to share in the American dream as a community?

First and foremost we need to start yesterday to repair the African-American community.

References

Wealth, Race and the Great Recession By MICHAEL POWELL
The New York Times July 26, 2011

Thomas Shapiro, "Institute on Assets and Social Policy" May
17, 2010

Alston, Lee J. and Joseph P. Ferrie. "Paternalism in Agricultural
Labor Contracts in the U.S. South:

Implications for the Growth of the Welfare State." American
Economic Review 83, no. 4 (1993): 852-76.

American Freedmen's Inquiry Commission. Records of the
American Freedmen's Inquiry Commission, Final Report, Senate
Executive Document 53, 38th Congress, 1st Session, Serial
1176, 1864.

Cimbala, Paul and Randall Miller. The Freedmen's Bureau and
Reconstruction: Reconsiderations. New York: Fordham
University Press, 1999.

Congressional Research Service,
http://clerk.house.gov/art_history/house_history/vetoes.html
Finley, Randy. From Slavery to Uncertain Freedom: The
Freedmen's Bureau in Arkansas, 1865-1869. Fayetteville:
University of Arkansas Press, 1996.

Johnson, Andrew. "Message of the President: Returning Bill
(S.60)," Pg. 3, 39th Congress, 1st Session, Executive Document
No. 25, February 19, 1866.

McFeely, William S. Yankee Stepfather: General O.O. Howard
and the Freedmen. New York: W.W. Norton, 1994.

Milton, George Fort. The Age of Hate: Andrew Johnson and the
Radicals. New York: Coward-McCann, 1930.

Nash, Howard P. Andrew Johnson: Congress and
Reconstruction. Rutherford, NJ: Fairleigh Dickinson University
Press, 1972.

Parker, Marjorie H. "Some Educational Activities of the
Freedmen's Bureau." Journal of Negro Education 23, no. 1
(1954): 9-21.

Q.A. Gillmore to Carl Schurz, July 27, 1865, Documents
Accompanying the Report of Major General Carl Schurz, Hilton
Head, SC.

Wahl, Jenny B. The Bondsman's Burden: An Economic Analysis
of the Common Law of Southern Slavery. New York:
Cambridge University Press, 1998.

Ruggles, Steven, Matthew Sobek, Trent Alexander, Catherine A.
Fitch, Ronald Goeken, Patricia Kelly Hall, Miriam King, and
Chad Ronnander. Integrated Public Use Microdata Series:
Version 3.0 [Machine-readable database]. Minneapolis, MN:
Minnesota Population Center [producer and distributor], 2004.

Shlomowitz, Ralph. "The Transition from Slave to Freedman
Labor Arrangements in Southern Agriculture, 1865-1870."
Journal of Economic History 39, no. 1 (1979): 333-36.

Shlomowitz, Ralph, "The Origins of Southern Sharecropping,"
Agricultural History 53, no. 3 (1979): 557-75.

Simpson, Brooks D. "Ulysses S. Grant and the Freedmen's
Bureau." In The Freedmen's Bureau and Reconstruction:
Reconsiderations, edited by Paul A. Cimbala and Randall M.
Miller. New York: Fordham University Press, 1999.

Citation: Troost, William. "Freedmen's Bureau". EH.Net
Encyclopedia, edited by Robert Whaples. June 5, 2008. URL
http://eh.net/encyclopedia/article/troost.freedmens.bureau
Surviving Jim Crow: In-Depth EssayBy Ronald L. F. Davis, Ph.
D.

The curse of Cromwell

Bacon, Nathaniel". The World Book Encyclopedia. World Book. 1992. pp. 18. ISBN 0-7166-0092-7.
African Americans and the American Labor Movement By James Gilbert Cassedy

Maloney, Thomas N. "Wage Compression and Wage Inequality between Black and White Males in the United States, 1940-1960."

Racial Discrimination and Redlining in Cities

In poor health: Supermarket redlining and urban nutrition, Elizabeth Eisenhauer, GeoJournal Volume 53,

How East New York Became a Ghetto by Walter Thabit. ISBN 0-8147-8267-1. Page 42.

Sagawa, Shirley; Segal, Eli (1999). Common Interest, Common Good: Creating Value Through Business and Social Sector Partnerships. Harvard Business Press. pp. 30. ISBN 0875848486. Retrieved 2010-01-04.

 Benjamin Quarles, The Negro in the American Revolution (Chapel Hill: University of North Carolina Press, 1961), i.

Michael Lanning, African Americans in the Revolutionary War (New York: Kensington, 2000), 177.

American Revolution — African Americans In The Revolutionary Period.

Gordon Wood, The American Revolution: A History (New York: Modern Library, 2002), 55.

World Book [1]

Thomas H. O'Connor, The Hub: Boston Past and Present (Boston: Northeastern University Press, 2001), p. 56.

Philip Foner, Blacks in the American Revolution (Westport, Conn.: Greenwood Press, 1976), 43.

Liberty! The American Revolution (Documentary) Episode II:Blows Must Decide: 1774-1776. ©1997 Twin Cities Public Television, Inc. ISBN 1-4157-0217-9

The Revolution's Black Soldiers by Robert A. Selig, Ph.D.

Alfred Hunt, Haiti's Influence on Antebellum America, p. 31

The Biology of Skin Color – HHMI Bio-Interactive Video, Dr. Nina Jablonski (Published July 20, 2015)

www.ingramcontent.com/pod-product-compliance
Lightning Source LLC
Chambersburg PA
CBHW060646280326
41933CB00012B/2178

* 9 780692 620113 *